Just the Facts
Capital
Punishment

Anne Rooney

Heinemann
LIBRARY

www.heinemann.co.uk/library
Visit our website to find out more information about **Heinemann Library** books.

To order:
 Phone 44 (0) 1865 888066
 Send a fax to 44 (0) 1865 314091
Visit the Heinemann Bookshop at www.heinemann.co.uk/library to browse our catalogue and order online.

Produced by Monkey Puzzle Media Ltd
Gissing's Farm, Fressingfield, Suffolk IP21 5SH, UK

First published in Great Britain by Heinemann Library, Halley Court, Jordan Hill, Oxford OX2 8EJ, part of Harcourt Education.
Heinemann is a registered trademark of Harcourt Education Ltd.

Editorial: Daniel Rogers, Sarah Eason and Louise Galpine
Design: Mayer Media Ltd
Picture Research: Lynda Lines and Frances Bailey
Consultant: Ian Derbyshire
Production: Duncan Gilbert

Originated by Ambassador Litho Ltd
Printed and bound in Hong Kong, China by South China Printing Company

ISBN 0 431 16176 3
09 08 07 06 05
10 9 8 7 6 5 4 3 2 1

British Library Cataloguing in Publication Data
Rooney, Anne
Capital Punishment
364.6'6
A full catalogue record for this book is available from the British Library.

Acknowledgements
The publishers would like to thank the following for permission to reproduce photographs:
AKG-Images pp. **8–9** (Rabatti-Domingie), **10**; Associated Press pp. **14** (Pat Sullivan), **25, 28** (Mark Foley), **43** (Boris Heger), **45** (Anat Givon); Corbis pp. **11** (Bettmann), **22** (Shepard Sherbell), **26** (Ralf-Finn Hestoft), **34** Alberto Pizzoli/Sygma), **38** (Mark Peterson), **46** (Ron Sachs); Florida Department of Corrections p. **5**; Getty Images pp. **13** (STR/AFP), **17** (Bay Ismoyo/AFP), **21** (Diana Walker/Time Life Pictures); PA Photos p. **33** (Rosie Hallam); Popperfoto.com p. **32**; Reuters pp. **29** (Daniel Leclair), **36** (Yves Herman), **41** (Jerry Lampen), **42** (Jamal Saidi), **47** (Sukree Sukplang), **48** (Juda Ngwenya); Rex Features pp. **4** (SIPA), **6** (SIPA), **7** (SIPA), **18** (SIPA), **23** (SIPA), **31**; Topham Picturepoint pp. **19** (James Nubile/Image Works), **24, 37** (Daemmrich/Image Works).

Cover photograph reproduced with permission of Associated Press (Mark Foley).

Every effort has been made to contact copyright holders of any material reproduced in this book. Any omissions will be rectified in subsequent printings if notice is given to the publishers.

Any words appearing in the text in bold, **like this**, are explained in the Glossary.

Contents

What is capital punishment?

What would happen to you if you committed a serious crime, such as murder? The answer will depend on where you live and who you are. In many places, serious criminals are imprisoned. In others, people found guilty of very serious crimes may be executed – killed as a punishment. Even children may be imprisoned or executed in some countries. The execution of criminals is called capital punishment.

After their trial, persons who have had a death sentence passed on them, (**condemned prisoners**) are usually taken to a prison and held in a special part, known as **death row**, until their execution. In some places, they can try to get their sentence changed by going through an **appeals** procedure, their lawyers presenting more evidence and arguments to defend them. Not all countries have a fair trial and appeals procedure, though. In some places, prisoners may be executed very soon after their **conviction** with no chance to appeal.

A noose used to hang men convicted of robbery and rape in Tehran, Iran in 2002.

Methods of execution

More than half the countries in the world have now abolished the death penalty, but several methods of execution are used by countries that do still have a death penalty. The methods used vary by country and in some the condemned prisoner is offered a choice of execution method.

Shooting is available as an execution method in 73 countries. It may be carried out by a **firing squad** or a single executioner. A firing squad consists of several **marksmen** who shoot at the prisoner all at the same time. Death should be instant, but if the prisoner is not killed, another shot is fired, usually at short range.

At the start of 2004, Utah, Oklahoma and Idaho are the only US states to allow death by shooting, and all use a firing squad. A firing squad was last used in the USA in Utah in 1996.

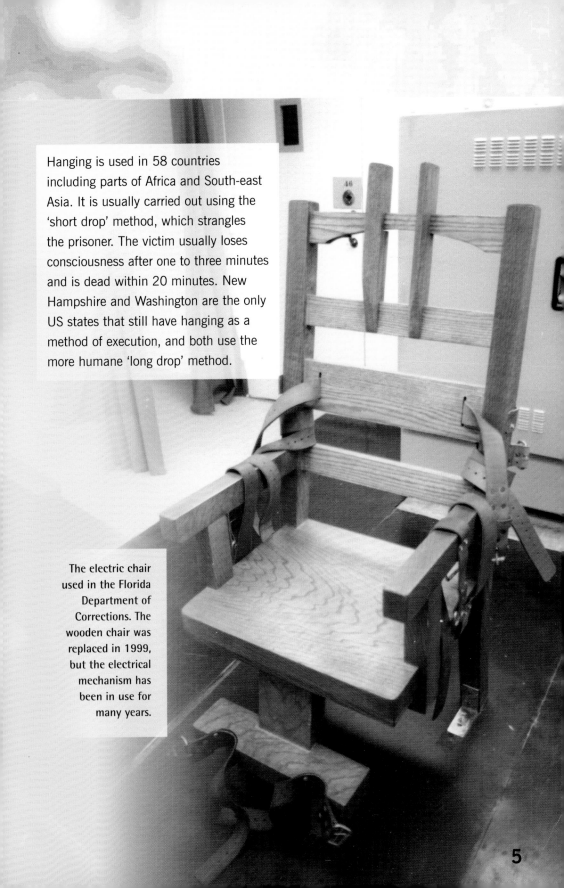

Hanging is used in 58 countries including parts of Africa and South-east Asia. It is usually carried out using the 'short drop' method, which strangles the prisoner. The victim usually loses consciousness after one to three minutes and is dead within 20 minutes. New Hampshire and Washington are the only US states that still have hanging as a method of execution, and both use the more humane 'long drop' method.

The electric chair used in the Florida Department of Corrections. The wooden chair was replaced in 1999, but the electrical mechanism has been in use for many years.

Electrocution is used only in the USA, where it is an available method in ten states. In Nebraska, it is the only method used. The condemned prisoner is strapped into an electric chair with one electrode attached to the leg and another inside a special helmet. A charge of 1700 to 2400 volts is applied for up to a minute. If this does not kill the prisoner a second and even further charges are applied. Some experts say that the prisoner loses consciousness in less than one hundredth of a second, but others say it may take up to 30 seconds. Death usually happens within a few minutes; paralysis stops the heart and breathing.

Lethal injection is widely used in the USA and China. The prisoner is strapped to a hospital trolley and tubes are inserted into a vein in each arm. A combination of three drugs is used: the first makes the victim unconscious, the second stops breathing and the third stops the heart. The victim usually loses consciousness about a minute after the first drug is injected and dies in around eight minutes. This method is used in 37 states in the USA, and by the US military and **federal** government.

The gas chamber can be used as a means of execution in the US states of Arizona, Maryland, Missouri and Wyoming – nowhere else uses it. The victim is strapped into a seat in a sealed chamber, and cyanide gas is produced by dropping sodium cyanide pellets into a bowl of sulphuric acid beneath the chair. Death is caused by lack of oxygen to the brain. The prisoner often loses consciousness in under three minutes, but some people take much longer to die and show signs of extreme pain during this time. Death takes around 20 minutes.

A prisoner in Saudi Arabia about to be beheaded with a sword. Saudi Arabian executioners take great pride in their work and the job is often passed from father to son.

6

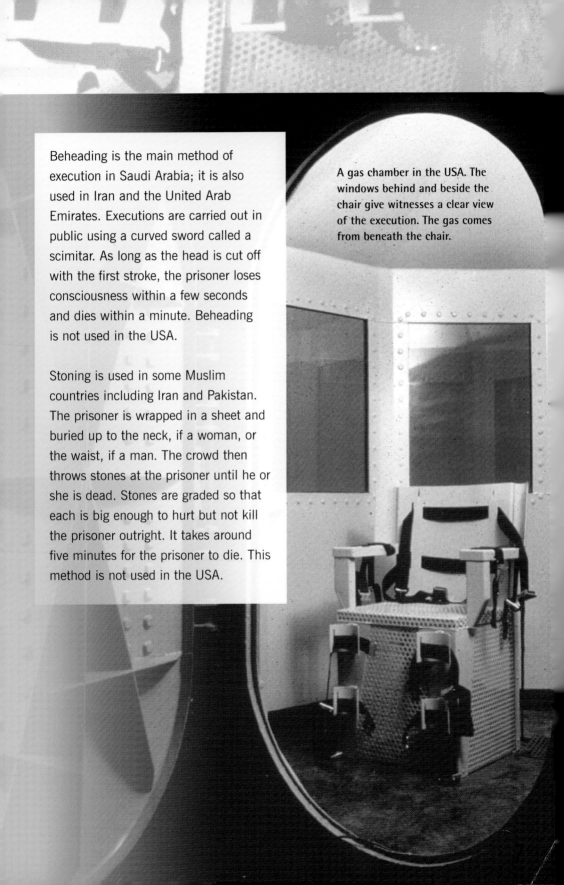

Beheading is the main method of execution in Saudi Arabia; it is also used in Iran and the United Arab Emirates. Executions are carried out in public using a curved sword called a scimitar. As long as the head is cut off with the first stroke, the prisoner loses consciousness within a few seconds and dies within a minute. Beheading is not used in the USA.

Stoning is used in some Muslim countries including Iran and Pakistan. The prisoner is wrapped in a sheet and buried up to the neck, if a woman, or the waist, if a man. The crowd then throws stones at the prisoner until he or she is dead. Stones are graded so that each is big enough to hurt but not kill the prisoner outright. It takes around five minutes for the prisoner to die. This method is not used in the USA.

A gas chamber in the USA. The windows behind and beside the chair give witnesses a clear view of the execution. The gas comes from beneath the chair.

A long history

Capital punishment has probably been used since the earliest human societies began, thousands of years ago. The first record we have of a death penalty is in the laws passed by King Hammurabi of Babylon nearly 4000 years ago. The laws list 25 crimes that were punishable by death.

Cruel treatment

Executions in the past have sometimes been very brutal, and sometimes quick and efficient. In some places, criminals have been thrown off a cliff, drowned in the local river or killed with a sword. Many societies have had periods of devising especially unpleasant and cruel deaths. Burning at the stake was used in much of Europe, and was used in England for **heretics** until 1790. Other societies around the world have exposed criminals to die in the cold or heat, to be eaten by wild animals or insects, or have inflicted other slow and painful deaths intended to increase their suffering.

A painless death?

In most parts of the world where a death penalty is still used, the death itself is thought to be sufficient punishment and is intended to be as quick and painless as possible. Criminals have been hanged or beheaded in Europe for many centuries, and hanging was used early in the settlement of America and Australia. Over the last two hundred years, authorities have looked for ways of making these methods less painful. Hanging was made more humane by the development of the 'long drop' method, which should break the

This painting from the 1460s shows Jews being burned at the stake for desecrating the host (the wine and wafer believed by Christians to be the blood and body of Christ).

prisoner's neck immediately. However, the short drop method is still widely used as it requires less preparation, expertise and equipment. Beheading by **guillotine** was intended to be more humane than using a sword or an axe.

Even so, modern methods of execution are not completely painless and some may inflict several minutes of physical suffering. Lethal injection, which is usually claimed to be least painful, involves considerable mental anguish for the prisoner. It takes around 45 minutes to strap down the prisoner and insert large tubes into his or her veins. As many **condemned** prisoners are **intravenous** drug abusers with damaged veins, inserting the tubes can be a long, difficult and painful procedure. Electrocution can go wrong, too, causing severe burning.

9

To die for

Where the death penalty is still used, it is generally kept for serious crimes, but this has not always been the case. When law enforcement was difficult, capital punishment was widely used even for quite minor crimes. It meant that criminals were removed from society immediately, and it dispensed with the complication of trying to run prisons.

Which crimes have been punishable by death has changed over time. In Britain in 1500, hanging was the usual punishment for **treason**, murder, robbery, rape and arson. Gradually, more and more crimes attracted the death penalty, some of them very petty. In 1699, shoplifting goods to the value of five shillings (25 pence) became a capital offence. Later, wearing a disguise while committing a crime was punishable by death. The pattern was the same in America and Australia.

Eventually, fewer people were convicted of crimes in these countries because **juries** thought the death penalty too harsh. Rather than let criminals go free, the law was changed to reduce the number of **capital offences**, and criminals were imprisoned, fined, deported, flogged or maimed instead.

Is it a crime?

Not everyone who has faced the death penalty has been a criminal in the modern sense of the word.

Many millions of people throughout history have been killed for their beliefs – for speaking out against their rulers, for following a particular religion or for trying to change the world they live in. A few centuries ago in Europe, people

❝If hanging was abolished for theft, the property of Englishmen would be left wholly without protection.❞

John Scott (Lord Eldon), British Lord Chancellor 1807–1827

could be killed for being Catholics in a Protestant country or Protestants in a Catholic country. In America, a slave could be killed for running away from slavery.

Throughout world history, political leaders have executed people who oppose them. In times of peace, rebels or opponents may be convicted of treason, which has carried the death sentence in most societies at some time. After a revolution or invasion, it has been common to kill the supporters of the leader who has been overthrown, to prevent further trouble.

In the past, many people have been executed for crimes that are no longer recognized – for witchcraft or **heresy**, for example. Many have been executed after confessing under **torture** to crimes they probably did not commit.

After a seven-month siege, the Dutch town of Haarlem surrendered to the Spanish in 1573. The Spanish massacred 1700 soldiers and citizens as 'punishment' for their opposition.

In 1692 in Salem, Massachusetts, USA, 25 people were executed for witchcraft. The executions followed a frenzy of accusations and dramatic trials at which the flimsiest evidence was accepted as proof.

Public and private executions

Until the middle of the 19th century, executions were usually carried out in public. They were often a great spectacle, drawing large crowds with a holiday atmosphere. In some countries, executions are still held in public.

For all to see

The main reason for holding public executions is to deter other potential criminals. The idea is that if people see what could happen to them, they might be less likely to commit crimes.

Public executions are usually more unpleasant for the **condemned** person. Societies that hold executions in private hold that the extra suffering is not acceptable or necessary; those that carry out public executions consider the additional distress caused to the prisoner is justified or is even part of the punishment.

Public executions may be used as a show of power, particularly if the rulers feel threatened or vulnerable. General Pinochet seized power in Chile in 1973 and ruled until 1990. He had thousands of people publicly executed to underline the strength of his new **regime** and to deter opponents.

Ritual

Executions were often symbolic in some way. In 16th-century Venice, a man who had stolen money from the state had his hand cut off and hung around his neck on a chain and was then beheaded with a sword. The removal of the hand 'punished' the part of the body symbolically guilty of the crime, cleansing the criminal. The beheading then cleansed the whole society by removing the criminal.

On display

It was common in many places to leave the prisoner's body on display as a warning to other people. In England, the heads of executed traitors were set on spikes on London Bridge. The bodies of hanged criminals were often left hanging from the **gallows** or **gibbet**. As well as acting as a lasting deterrent, this prevented burial, which some believed was necessary before the spirit could move on to the next world, and so was an extra punishment.

> **"**His body being weak with the **torture** and sickness he was scarce able to go up the ladder, yet, with much ado, by the help of the hangman, went high enough to break his neck by the fall ... to the great joy of all beholders that the land was ended of so wicked a villainy.**"**
>
> Report of the execution of Guy Fawkes, Weekely Newes, 31 January 1606

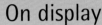

Executions are often carried out in large sports stadiums in China. Here, police parade condemned prisoners before shooting them.

13

Capital punishment around the world

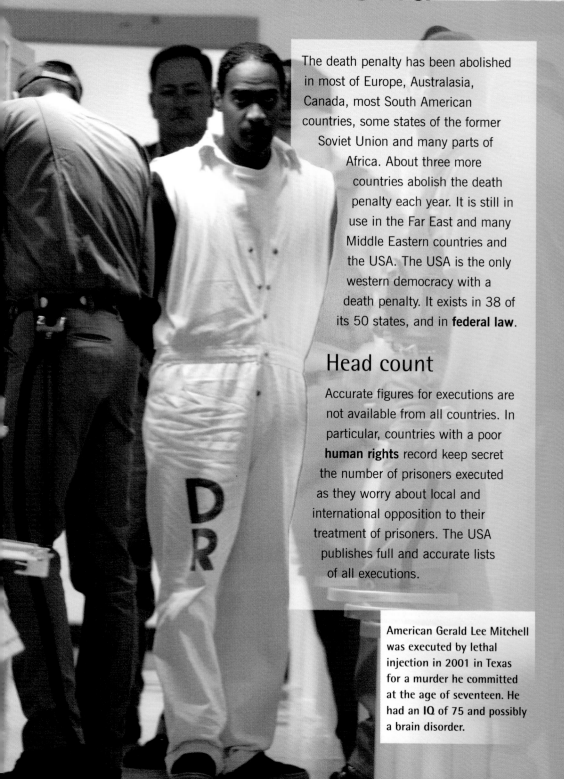

The death penalty has been abolished in most of Europe, Australasia, Canada, most South American countries, some states of the former Soviet Union and many parts of Africa. About three more countries abolish the death penalty each year. It is still in use in the Far East and many Middle Eastern countries and the USA. The USA is the only western democracy with a death penalty. It exists in 38 of its 50 states, and in **federal law**.

Head count

Accurate figures for executions are not available from all countries. In particular, countries with a poor **human rights** record keep secret the number of prisoners executed as they worry about local and international opposition to their treatment of prisoners. The USA publishes full and accurate lists of all executions.

American Gerald Lee Mitchell was executed by lethal injection in 2001 in Texas for a murder he committed at the age of seventeen. He had an IQ of 75 and possibly a brain disorder.

Child executions

International human rights law makes it illegal to execute children, which it defines as anyone under the age of eighteen when they committed their crime. The **United Nations** Covenant on Civil and Political Rights (1976), which sets out this law, has been accepted by all countries that are members of the United Nations except the USA and Somalia.

The USA ruled in 1993 that the execution of anyone who was under sixteen years old at the time of their crime is **unconstitutional**. Twenty-two states still allow the execution of people who were sixteen or seventeen years old when they committed their crimes.

"Sentence of death shall not be imposed for crimes committed by persons below eighteen years of age."

Article 6, The United Nations International Covenant on Civil and Political Rights, 1976

A dying practice?

- 83 countries still have a death penalty, though in many it is rarely used
- 76 have abolished it completely
- 15 have a death penalty in exceptional circumstances, such as during war
- 21 are 'abolitionist in practice' – they have not used the death penalty in ten years and are known to have a policy of avoiding it.

Executions in 2002

China: 1,060 plus
(probably many more, and maybe as many as 10,000)
Iran: 113 plus
USA: 71

Source: Amnesty International

Executions of people under 18 at the time of their crime, 1994–2003

USA: 13
Iran: 3
Pakistan: 2
Congo: 1
Nigeria: 1

Crimes that attract capital punishment

The **United Nations** insists that the death penalty be used 'only for the most serious crimes' and that it should be carried out humanely.

In many countries that still have a death penalty, the death sentence is reserved for the most serious crimes, such as murder and terrorism, but this is not the case everywhere.

The death penalty in the USA

In the USA, the death penalty may be passed down to murderers, to criminals who kill while carrying out some other crimes (such as kidnapping or sex crimes) and for spying, **treason** or running a large-scale drug trafficking operation. The law varies in different states. Although twelve states do not have a death penalty, a **federal** death penalty can be invoked (called into use) for some offences.

Crack-down on crime

Countries that have difficulty maintaining law and order, or want to crack down hard on crime, often use the death penalty for less serious crimes. China is currently using the death penalty extensively to try to stem rising crime under its 'Strike Hard' campaign started in 1996.

In China, crimes such as theft, hooliganism, sexual harassment, tax or insurance **fraud** and even 'passing on methods of committing crimes' can bring a death penalty. Many people are sentenced and executed after quick and possibly unfair trials and have no right to **appeal** against their sentence. Executions are often carried out in public, prisoners being shot in sports stadiums in front of large crowds.

GRANAT

> **"No one shall be subjected to torture or to cruel, inhuman or degrading treatment or punishment."**
>
> Article 5, Universal Declaration of Human Rights, 1948

In South-east Asian countries where drug smuggling is a serious problem, the death penalty is often imposed for this crime.

Shari'a law

In some countries, the death penalty is part of a legal code based on religious belief. Shari'a law is a moral code of living for Muslims, based on the holy text the Qur'an. It includes a set of penalties for specific crimes, called Hadd offences. Elements of Shari'a law are included in the legal system of some Islamic countries in the Middle East and Africa, including Saudi Arabia, Sudan, Libya, Iran and Nigeria. Shari'a law demands harsh penalties for some offences that are not considered crimes elsewhere. There have been highly publicized cases recently of women being **condemned** to death by stoning for **adultery**.

Dutch woman Sibel Yalvac, who was arrested for possession of ecstasy tablets at Jakarta International Airport, Indonesia, in 2003. Drug smuggling and trafficking can be punishable by death in Indonesia.

Capital punishment and the legal system

In the 7th century BCE, the Draconian Code – a **legal code** put together by the Athenian ruler Draco in ancient Greece – made the death penalty the only punishment for all crimes. Now, the legal codes of all societies provide a range of punishments, which may sometimes include capital punishment.

Death or prison?

Many countries have a prison system and often **non-custodial punishments** that do not involve going to prison. For example, people who have committed relatively minor crimes in a country such as the UK or the USA may have to pay a fine, or perhaps carry out work in the community to recompense society for their crimes.

Prisons in the developed world aim to be hygienic and safe – the punishment lies in being separated from normal life, friends and family. Elsewhere, prison conditions are sometimes appalling, with filthy, overcrowded cells plagued by rats, cockroaches and fleas. Prisoners may have inadequate food and medical attention, or little access to fresh air and exercise. Many fall ill and die. This treatment contravenes international law, but is common.

In countries with no death penalty, imprisonment is the most severe

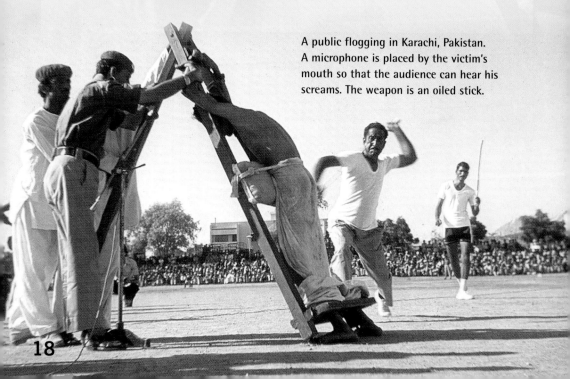

A public flogging in Karachi, Pakistan. A microphone is placed by the victim's mouth so that the audience can hear his screams. The weapon is an oiled stick.

Convicted criminals in Connecticut, USA, shovel snow as part of a community service programme. This is an alternative to a jail term and it benefits the local community, too.

punishment available. For serious crimes, the sentence may be 'life'. In the UK and Australia, a limit is generally set on the term of life imprisonment. In the USA, someone may be imprisoned for the whole of the rest of their life with no hope of **parole**.

> **❝What comparison can there really be ... between consigning a man to the short pang of a rapid death, and immuring [imprisoning] him in a living tomb...?❞**
>
> John Stuart Mill, speaking in the UK parliament, 1868

Discretionary and mandatory sentences

A death penalty may be **discretionary** or **mandatory**. If it is mandatory, the judge has no choice but to condemn a person convicted of that crime. If it is discretionary, the judge may choose to inflict the death penalty or another punishment.

Corporal punishment

Some countries, including those that have a legal code embracing Shari'a law, use other forms of physical punishment as well as capital punishment. The most common of these **corporal punishments** are flogging and amputation of fingers, hands or feet.

Torture

Torture is deliberately inflicting pain on someone, usually with the aim of getting them to give up information. It is illegal under international **human rights** law, but is carried out in prisons and by the military in many countries. Sometimes victims may be tortured before execution, or tortured to death if they do not provide the information the torturers want.

Death row

Prisoners who have been **condemned** to death are usually kept in prison until their execution. In some countries, the execution may be very soon after the trial, or the prisoner may even be taken straight to the place of execution. In other countries, there may be a considerable delay before the execution.

Prisoners awaiting execution are often kept in a special part of the prison called 'death row'. In the USA, prisoners on death row can usually watch television, read, write and consult legal materials and lawyers. They are given sufficient food, kept warm and allowed some exercise. Some prisoners are allowed to work. In other parts of the world, conditions vary, but are often very poor.

How long?

In the USA, prisoners may spend a long time on death row as their lawyers lodge **appeals** to have their sentence changed. There were 3517 prisoners on death row in the USA at 1 August 2003. The average stay for a prisoner on death row in Texas (the state with most condemned prisoners) is just over 10 years.

In other countries, prisoners may be executed without notice, and without a chance to say goodbye to their families. Prisoners in Japan and Thailand may be executed at any point once they have been sentenced and their appeals have failed. Even so, some countries in South-east Asia have sophisticated appeals procedures and prisoners may remain on death row in terrible conditions for many years.

Psychological torture

Even when the physical conditions on death row are sufficient to keep prisoners healthy, the stress of waiting for death, sometimes for years, causes great emotional strain. Boredom, anxiety, fear of death and the pointlessness of life while waiting to die often lead to psychological problems. Where conditions are bad as well, despair and ill-health are common. Many prisoners attempt suicide, or express a desire to kill themselves.

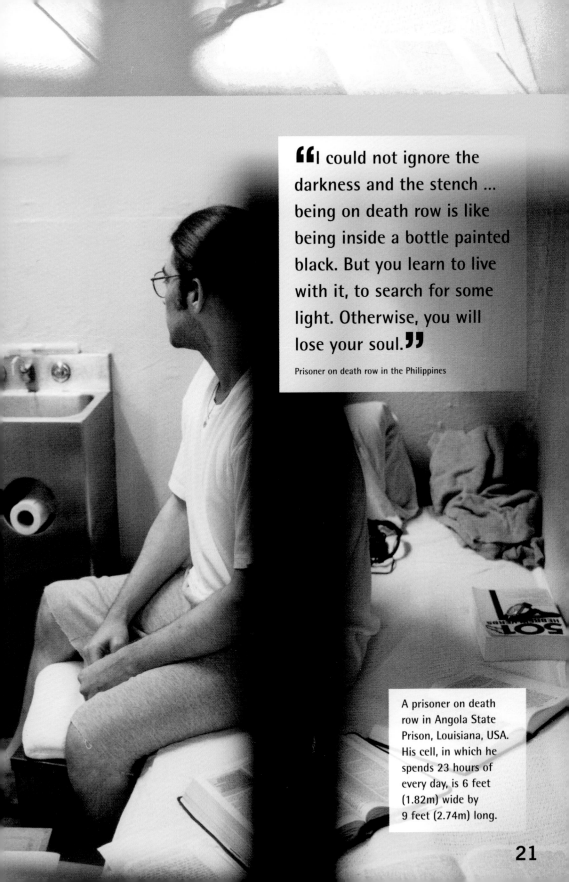

"I could not ignore the darkness and the stench ... being on death row is like being inside a bottle painted black. But you learn to live with it, to search for some light. Otherwise, you will lose your soul."

Prisoner on death row in the Philippines

A prisoner on death row in Angola State Prison, Louisiana, USA. His cell, in which he spends 23 hours of every day, is 6 feet (1.82m) wide by 9 feet (2.74m) long.

A day in the death of...

Exactly what it is like on death row as a **condemned** prisoner varies from one place to another. This is what a prisoner in the USA can expect, where the conditions are better than elsewhere.

The long haul

A cell on Florida's death row measures 6 feet by 9 feet (1.82m by 2.74m), with solid walls on three sides and iron bars on the fourth side. There is a bed, a toilet and a washbasin. Inmates may have a radio and a television, but must provide these themselves. They spend all their time alone in the cells, except for showering (every other day), exercise and rare visits by friends or relatives. Whenever prisoners are outside their cells, they must wear handcuffs; these are taken off for exercise and showers. Meals are served in the cells, with a plate and spoon only. Death row prisoners wear special clothes to distinguish them from other prisoners.

Countdown to execution

When an execution date is set, the prisoner is told and arrangements begin. Prisoners can choose some of the witnesses to the execution, usually including spiritual advisors, lawyers and adult friends or relatives.

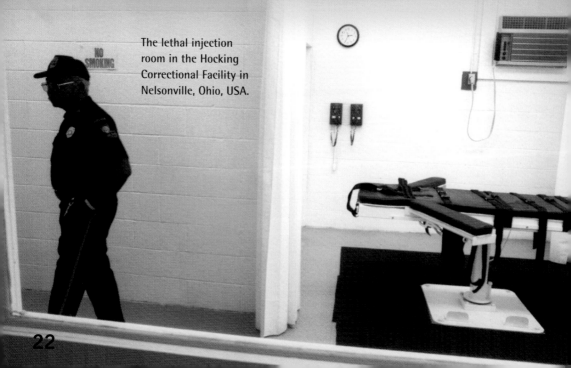

The lethal injection room in the Hocking Correctional Facility in Nelsonville, Ohio, USA.

Prison guards make their rounds on death row in the Arizona Department of Corrections, Phoenix, Arizona, USA.

The prison may nominate up to eight victims or relatives of victims and ten members of the press to be witnesses.

In the last week, the prisoner chooses his or her last meal. The prison buys the chemicals for the lethal injection, if this is the method of execution. Between 48 and 24 hours before execution, the prisoner is moved to the death watch cell, often in a different building.

Death watch

Death watch officers stay with the prisoner at all times to prevent suicide or escape attempts. There are last visits and phone calls, and the final meal is served. The prisoner is **strip-searched** and has to dress in special clothes. Prisoners who will be electrocuted are shaved, to allow better electrical contact.

Eventually, the prisoner walks to the execution chamber, sometimes wearing handcuffs and leg irons. There he or she is strapped into the electric chair or to a hospital trolley and can make a final statement. The witnesses sit in an adjoining room with a window onto the execution chamber. At the appointed time, the prisoner is executed.

War and illegal regimes

A **firing squad** executes a soldier on the Western Front during World War I.

Attitudes towards capital punishment are different in war time, and in many places different laws apply during a war. Armies are often allowed to shoot deserters – soldiers who run away from battle – and civilians may be executed for working with or spying for the enemy.

Court martials

During wars, people may be executed after only a short trial by a military court and with no chance to **appeal** against their sentence. A military court operates in a different way and following different laws from a civilian court. During World War I (1914–18), for instance, over 3000 British soldiers were executed for **desertion**, cowardice, or falling asleep at their post.

International law sets out how soldiers and governments may behave during war. War crimes are crimes carried out during a war, often by soldiers following illegal orders from senior officers or their government. Recent reports of war crimes include the execution of ethnic Albanians in Kosovo (a province of Serbia) and the execution of Kuwaiti prisoners of war by Iraqi troops in 1991. The execution of prisoners of war is illegal under the Geneva Convention (1949), an international code that sets out how prisoners of war must be treated.

During World War II (1939–45), Nazi German authorities in occupied countries such as France, Belgium and Poland ordered the public execution of people who had been working to overthrow the German forces in their country. They often executed young women, usually by hanging them. This was intended to dissuade other people from fighting against the Germans. Although the killings were ordered by the Nazi government of the time, they were illegal under international law. Some of the soldiers responsible for these and other crimes – including the mass slaughter of Jews, homosexuals and mentally ill people in the concentration camps – were tried by an international court after the war. (Concentration camps were detention centres set up to hold and often execute large numbers of people the Nazi rulers considered undesirable.)

Revolution

During or after a revolution, and in countries that are politically unstable, people who oppose the rulers may be executed even if their own protest is peaceful. A government that has seized power and carries out killings that are illegal under international law is often called an illegal regime. Other countries may avoid dealing with an illegal regime, but often this isolation leads to even worse **atrocities**.

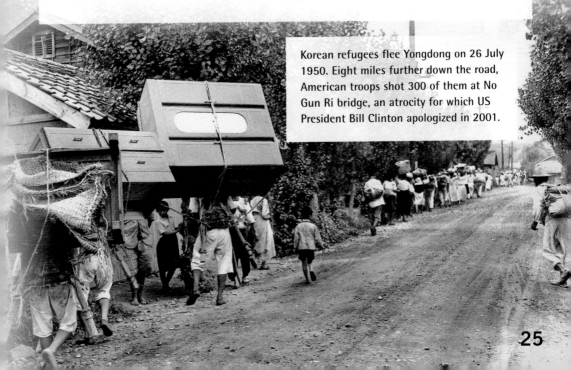

Korean refugees flee Yongdong on 26 July 1950. Eight miles further down the road, American troops shot 300 of them at No Gun Ri bridge, an atrocity for which US President Bill Clinton apologized in 2001.

In the news

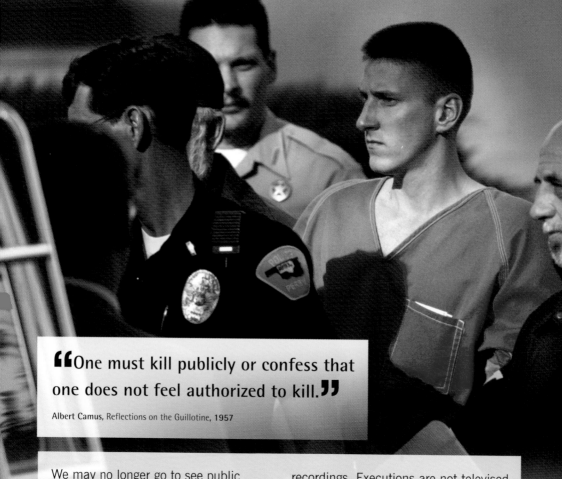

"One must kill publicly or confess that one does not feel authorized to kill."

Albert Camus, Reflections on the Guillotine, 1957

We may no longer go to see public executions, but should we be able to watch them – perhaps on television or online?

The law in the USA

In the USA, executions are carried out inside prisons with a room set aside for witnesses, including journalists. Reporters are allowed to write about the execution but they are not allowed to take in still or video cameras or make recordings. Executions are not televised, though there have been requests that they should be.

The rest of the world

Executions are televised in some countries. Chechnya has televised executions, including that of a murderer who had his throat slit. Other countries that have televised executions are Afghanistan, Thailand, Russia, China, Nigeria, Iraq, Vietnam, Saudi Arabia,

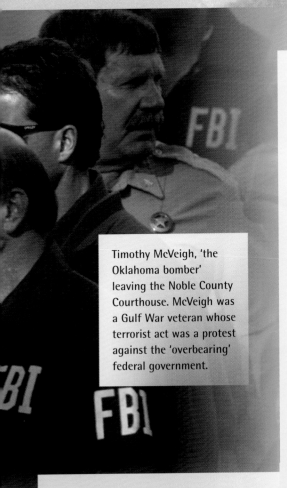

Timothy McVeigh, 'the Oklahoma bomber' leaving the Noble County Courthouse. McVeigh was a Gulf War veteran whose terrorist act was a protest against the 'overbearing' federal government.

Case study
The execution of Timothy McVeigh

Timothy McVeigh was **convicted** of planting a bomb at the Murrah **federal** building in Oklahoma in 1995 which killed 186 people. His execution in 2001 by lethal injection was shown by closed circuit television to 330 survivors of the bombing and relatives of the victims.

Before the execution, Entertainment Network Inc (ENI) asked to be allowed to broadcast it on the web, charging US$1.95 to be paid by credit card. They were not allowed to. Campaigners both for and against the death penalty supported the move to televise the execution. Others on both sides argued against it. (McVeigh had asked that his execution be broadcast, so violation of his privacy was not an issue.) Some people felt it barbaric to broadcast an execution; others felt it would work better as a deterrent if people could see it. The prison authorities were worried that other prisoners would riot if the execution was broadcast and seen as entertainment or sport by the public. Others worried that McVeigh would use the opportunity to present himself as a martyr.

Kazakhstan, and Romania under Nicolae Ceausescu's tyrannical **regime** (1974–89).

In Guatemala in 1996, two men convicted of raping and murdering a child were executed by **firing squad** in a televised execution. The firing squad failed to kill one man, who had to be shot again. The broadcast was repeated both within Guatemala and around the world, including the USA. It led to Guatemala adopting lethal injection as a 'more humane' method of execution.

Does it work?

Countries that still have a death penalty may defend it in several ways:
- it deters potential criminals
- it prevents a criminal from re-offending
- it helps the family of the victim achieve **closure**.

Opponents of the death penalty argue that it does not work as a deterrent and that revenge is not morally acceptable, even if called closure. (Many psychologists believe people need a formal end to a bad period in their lives before they can properly grieve and move on to a more positive state.

They call this ending closure.) They do not deny that it stops the criminal re-offending.

Statistics speak

Legal systems around the world and through time have tried to come up with punishment systems that deter criminals. There is much debate about whether the death penalty does genuinely reduce crime.

The crime which is most often punished by death in the USA is murder. *The New York Times* reported in 2000 that ten of the twelve states without the death penalty have murder rates below the national average. Typically, the murder rate in states with the death penalty has been 50–100 per cent higher than in states without the death penalty. It has been found around the world that the number of murders does not increase when a country abolishes the death penalty. This would suggest that capital punishment is no better as a deterrent than life imprisonment. Many murders are carried out on the spur of the moment, and many murderers do not try to get away with or deny their crimes, so for them no punishment would have a deterrent effect.

Prisoners on death row in Florida State Prison, Starke, Florida in the USA.

A car window, riddled with bullet holes during a fatal shooting in San Pedro Sula, Honduras. Rising crime has led to calls for the death penalty to be reintroduced.

❝An opinion seems to prevail that the death penalty is essential to the maintenance of law and order, justifiable against singularly heinous offences, and a vital deterrent against escalation of crime. This appears to be disproved by the experience of the countries which have abolished capital punishment.❞

Kurt Waldheim, Secretary General of the United Nations, 1980

There are many factors that affect the crime rate anywhere. Some people would argue that the existence of a death penalty brutalizes people, so they are more likely to commit violent crimes. They say that continued exposure to violence and cruelty reduces people's sensitivity, makes them more tolerant of violence and more likely to commit it themselves. Others would say that the death penalty is retained in states and countries where the population is more violent anyway – perhaps because of poverty or other types of social injustice – and that the murder rate would be even higher without it.

Social and economic costs

In the past, execution was a quick and easy way to deal with criminals when societies were unable to imprison them. These days, imprisonment is a realistic alternative in most places – and may even be cheaper than executions.

How much does it cost?

In some countries, execution is still the cheap option. In China, for example, there is little or no **appeals** procedure, and a prisoner may be executed within a few days or even hours of being found guilty. Yet in a country with a sophisticated legal system and good appeals procedure, execution can be more expensive than life imprisonment. In the USA, it costs an average of US$750,000 to keep someone in prison for life, but US$2.5 million or more to execute them because of the costly appeals process. Only 11 per cent of the people sentenced to death since 1978 in the USA have been executed, but every prisoner on death row costs around US$2 million as their appeals are all processed.

Social impact

People who argue in favour of capital punishment say that society and the victims of crime can heal better if the criminal has been executed, and that a death penalty shows that people totally reject the behaviour of the criminal. They believe it is fair that someone who has taken a life should lose their own life in exchange. Some also say that execution is more humane than a life spent in prison with no hope of release.

People who argue against the death penalty say that society is made more brutal by executions, whether in private or in public. They say that killing cannot be used as a means of getting across

the message that killing is not acceptable. Many are also worried that the justice system is unfairly biased against some groups in society, and that innocent people can be executed.

Occasionally, execution may further someone's cause or aims. An executed prisoner may draw so much attention to him- or herself that they attract admirers or even imitators. A martyr is someone killed or persecuted for beliefs they will not give up. People who commit crimes because of a belief they hold may be seen as martyrs. It is easier for a criminal to achieve the status of a martyr if they are killed than if they are imprisoned. The Oklahoma bomber, Timothy McVeigh (see page 27) saw himself as a martyr to a cause. In the UK, where there is no death penalty, **IRA** member Bobby Sands starved himself to death in prison in 1981 and was seen by supporters as a martyr.

4

The trial of John Allen Muhammad, accused of shooting ten people from his car in Washington, USA, in 2002. He was sentenced to death, but a lengthy and costly appeals process is likely.

Killing the innocent

There have always been miscarriages of justice – cases when someone who is not guilty is convicted of a crime and punished for it. Countries in the developed world try hard to avoid miscarriages of justice and to give prisoners every chance to prove themselves innocent after they have been convicted, usually through an **appeals** procedure.

Many people who oppose capital punishment give the risk of executing someone who is not guilty as one of the reasons. If someone is imprisoned for something they did not do, they can later be released and compensated in some way for what they have suffered.

But if they have been executed, it is too late to reverse the punishment.

Too late

In Britain, Timothy Evans was hanged in 1950 for the murder of his wife and child, murders actually committed by his landlord, the serial killer John Christie. Christie was later found guilty of the murders and hanged in 1953, and Evans was pardoned posthumously (after his death), in 1966. The death penalty was suspended in Britain in 1965 largely as a result of this case.

In the USA, there is no process for re-examining a conviction after a prisoner has been executed, so no one can be

Derek Bentley being driven away from Croydon Crown Court, UK in November 1952. Bentley was executed for his part in an armed robbery in which a policeman was shot dead, but he was pardoned 45 years later.

pardoned after their death. The view of the US Supreme Court is that the appeals procedure is sufficient to avoid serious miscarriages of justice.

Anthony Porter was sentenced to death in Illinois for two murders in 1982. Fifty hours before his death he was granted a **stay of execution** on the grounds that his **IQ** was so low (51) that he did not understand what was happening. A group of journalism students took on his case and proved his innocence. He was released in 1999. Alstory Simon confessed to the murders and was sentenced to thirty-seven and a half years in prison.

In many countries, there is little or no chance of an innocent person being freed before execution as there is either no appeals procedure or an inadequate procedure.

Recently, **DNA** evidence has been used to show the innocence of some convicted prisoners. Some countries now require the police to collect and keep DNA evidence from crime scenes. In some places, including parts of the USA, DNA evidence cannot be used in cases of crimes committed before the law allowed DNA evidence, even if the evidence would prove the person's innocence.

Overturned

In 1999, 75 per cent of the death-penalty cases brought to appeal in Florida had the sentence overturned; 50 per cent of cases are overturned at the first appeal hearing, where no new evidence is presented.

On average, around five innocent people are released from **death row** in the USA every year.

There are no figures for innocent people actually executed, as a case is closed in the USA once someone has been executed for a crime. There can be no further investigation, even if new evidence is uncovered.

Scotsman Kenny Richey has been on death row in Ohio, USA since 1986 for a murder he denies committing. Amnesty International has called his case 'one of the most compelling cases of innocence **human rights** campaigners have ever seen.'

Moral arguments

Are we ever justified in taking the life of another person? Those who support capital punishment believe that we are; those who oppose it think that we are not.

Some people base their views and arguments in their religion. Some religions approve of a death penalty and others do not. The Bible can be used to argue either case and has been used by both sides of the debate. The Pope recently denounced capital punishment on behalf of the Catholic Church, though Mormons and many American Protestants are in favour of it. Capital punishment is also permitted under Islamic law.

> **"An eye for an eye and a tooth for a tooth leaves the whole world blind and toothless."**
>
> Mahatma Gandhi (1869–1948), pacifist and a leader of the struggle for India's independence from Britain

A life for a life

People who oppose the death penalty often argue that we all reduce ourselves to the same level as murderers by using capital punishment. Others maintain that if someone takes a life it is only fair that they should lose theirs in turn.

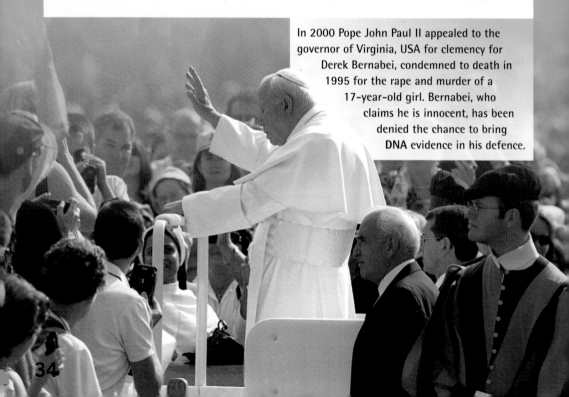

In 2000 Pope John Paul II appealed to the governor of Virginia, USA for clemency for Derek Bernabei, condemned to death in 1995 for the rape and murder of a 17-year-old girl. Bernabei, who claims he is innocent, has been denied the chance to bring DNA evidence in his defence.

In September 2003, a former Presbyterian minister, Paul Hill, was executed in Florida by lethal injection for the murder of a doctor. The doctor provided abortions, which Hill disapproved of and considered to be the murder of unborn children. Hill did not regret the murder, but saw it as the justifiable 'execution' of a man he saw as a murderer. Hill did not oppose his own execution – just as he thought the doctor should die for killing babies, he thought he himself should die for killing the doctor.

The executioners

Our attention naturally focuses on the **condemned** person who is executed – but what of the executioner? A death penalty requires that someone, or some group of people, must be responsible for killing another person.

In earlier centuries, a condemned prisoner could be freed in exchange for acting as executioner. Today, executioners are often recruited from the prison staff. In the USA, no one is forced to serve on a death watch team and be involved in executions.

Executioners in the USA are provided with counselling if they want it.

Research shows many executioners do not think about the moral issue of what they are doing, believing that as they are doing it for the state they bear no guilt. But some worry that they may suffer emotional damage, perhaps later in life.

❝Sometime I might wonder whether some day, after I retire, this here might come back and hit me in the face. Religious, like. When I'm an old man, ready to die, maybe this here will haunt me. I don't think it will, but it could...❞

Executioner, USA

❝I believe that the moment I'm executed, that my soul will be made perfect in holiness, and I will be in the immediate presence of the Lord, and I will be forever with him. So I'm looking forward to that.❞

Paul Hill, 2003

One moral law?

A mock stoning staged in Brussels by the National Council of Resistance of Iran to protest against executions by stoning in Iran.

Where morality is linked with religion, there can be immense problems in trying to change attitudes or practices; some people say we have no right to try. In recent years, much international pressure has been exerted to try to prevent executions by stoning in Nigeria. Most people living in modern democracies consider this a barbaric punishment. Yet the Muslims who defend this form of execution do so on the grounds of their religious beliefs. Does one group have a right to say their moral code is 'better' or more correct than another's?

What the people want

Most developed countries no longer have a death penalty, but in many of them the majority of the population is still in favour of capital punishment. Often, calls to restore the death penalty come after particularly horrific crimes which inspire emotion and a desire for

Few people would now defend some of the more barbaric executions carried out in the past. But is it fair to assume that what we decide is morally right in our own country should apply to other societies and cultures also? Some people believe that there is a single moral law that applies everywhere – others think that what is morally acceptable varies from one society and culture to another.

revenge – generally reaching a peak when a highly publicized murderer is on trial. The ruling group has imposed its own view – that the death penalty is bad – in spite of the view of the people who elect them. This has not happened in the USA. The judges and other officials involved in the day-to-day administration of the law there are often elected to their offices, so they are more directly accountable to the public.

Some people feel that elected politicians should act on the wishes and beliefs of the people who voted for them. Others feel that politicians should act for what they think is best for society as a whole. They argue that we have elected them to make decisions on our behalf to prevent self-interest dictating policy – after all, few people would choose to pay higher taxes, even though this may be necessary to create the kind of society they would like to live in.

Campaigners for the death penalty in Huntsville, Texas, USA. The placard refers to the convicted killer Karla Faye Tucker, executed in 1998 for her part in the murder of two people using a pickaxe.

Who is dying?

Some American states have reintroduced chain gangs as a punishment. These prisoners from Limestone Correctional Facility, Alabama are breaking rocks while chained together.

In most countries that have a death penalty, most of the people who are executed are poor or disadvantaged in some way. The country that provides most reliable figures in this respect is the USA. In the USA, a disproportionate number of inmates on death row are black or Hispanic, come from very poor backgrounds and have a very low level of intelligence and education. Of the people on death row in the USA in 2002, nearly 43 per cent were black, while only 11 per cent of the general population is black. In July 2003, there were 49 women on death row, only 1.4 per cent of **condemned** prisoners.

The people on death row

There are many reasons why the balance of the prison population, and in particular the population of death row, does not match the balance of the population in general. One reason is that people who are poor and

> **"Our capital system is haunted by the demon of error: error in determining guilt and error in determining who among the guilty deserves to die. What effect was race having? What effect was poverty having?"**
>
> Governor George Ryan on changing all Illinois death sentences to imprisonment, January 2003, affecting 156 death row prisoners

don't understand the **appeals** process and suffer because of errors in the **judicial** system which are not spotted or corrected by their lawyers.

Is it fair?

The death penalty was suspended in the USA in 1972 because the Supreme Court decided that it was administered in an arbitrary way – whether or not someone would die depended on many other factors than just the nature of the crime they had committed. This suspension was lifted in 1976 after laws were re-worded in several states. It is still the case that while some murderers are sentenced to death, many more are imprisoned for life or long periods.

ill-educated may be more likely to commit crimes in the first place, because they need money, and because they are angry and resentful at their lot in life. Another is that people who do not understand the law themselves, and cannot afford very good legal representation, will stand less chance of defending themselves during a trial than a richer, better-educated **defendant.** Everyone is entitled to a lawyer to defend them – but the best lawyers rarely take these cases. Many prisoners

The penalty imposed on a criminal in the USA will depend on state law. The same crime will be punished differently in Texas (which has the highest number of executions) and in Minnesota (which has no death penalty). The outcome of the trial will also depend on the quality of the prisoner's defence lawyers and the view of the **jury**, who are not legally trained. Anthony Porter (see page 33), was released from death row after an appeal found him innocent. The man who then confessed to the murders was not sentenced to death but imprisoned.

International agreements

Many countries that have a death penalty have a very poor **human rights** record: they may use **torture**, trials or **appeals** may be unfair, and prisoners may be badly treated. Organizations around the world are concerned with who is executed, how they are executed, how they are treated before execution, and how reliable and fair the legal process is. However, the death penalty is set by local laws in individual countries. In some places, such as the USA, there is further regional variation, with some states having a death penalty and others not. There is no global government making laws for everyone or seeing that international agreements are kept.

The United Nations

The **United Nations** is an international body with representatives from 191 countries. It was set up in 1945 with the aim of tackling problems that face the whole world. It acts to try to keep peace, combat disease, protect the environment, help developing countries and set basic standards for human rights around the world. Regarding the death penalty, the UN states that it must be used humanely and only for very serious crimes. This ruling is enshrined in international law in The International Bill of Human Rights (1948). The practice in some countries clearly contravenes this ruling, but the UN does not have any automatic method of enforcing the law.

The Council of Europe

The 44 member states of the Council of Europe agreed in 2002 to abolish the death penalty in all circumstances (it was already abolished in peace time). Any further countries that wish to join the Council of Europe will have to give up the death penalty if they still have it. Turkey has already had to forego the death penalty in order to support its application to join the European Union.

War and the Geneva Convention

Many executions are carried out during wars. The Geneva Convention (1949), put together after World War II, sets out how prisoners of war must be treated, and bans their execution or torture. There are now international tribunals set up to investigate illegal executions during war time, including **genocide**.

"The following acts are and shall remain prohibited at any time and in any place ... The passing of sentences and the carrying out of executions without previous judgment pronounced by a regularly constituted court affording all the judicial guarantees which are recognized as indispensable by civilized peoples."

The Geneva Convention, Article 3

Bosnian Serbs accused of war crimes in the former Yugoslavia in 1992–98 sit behind their defence lawyers at a hearing of the International War Crimes Tribunal at The Hague, Netherlands.

International pressure

There are several ways in which the international community can put pressure on countries with a poor **human rights** record.

Trade sanctions

All countries depend on international trade. They need to sell their goods to the outside world, and buy things that they cannot produce themselves from other countries. When the international community disapproves of a country's behaviour, it can impose trade sanctions. This means limiting what can be bought from and sold to the country. If a country depends on sales of oil, for instance, refusing to buy the oil will make life very difficult for the government of that country. However, politicians argue over whether trade sanctions may isolate a country further, have no effect on the ruling government but make life difficult for the people living there.

Political pressure

Sometimes, other kinds of political pressure can be brought to bear on a country considered to have a bad record in human rights. It can be left out of international bodies, and have aid payments or other international help restricted. Recently, Nigeria has been excluded from some international sporting events because of its cruel treatment of prisoners, including execution by stoning. By embarrassing the government of Nigeria, other countries hope to change the way it treats its people.

An oil refinery in Basrah, Iraq. Refusing to buy oil from a country is one way of putting pressure on a regime.

Security forces guard contestants in the Miss World competition in Nigeria in 2002. Religious tensions around the event within Nigeria, and international hostility towards Nigerian executions by stoning, made the contest a high-profile and volatile occasion.

In 1999, Russia and the Ukraine were threatened with expulsion from the Council of Europe unless they abandoned the death penalty. They had agreed to rule against it, but continued executions in secret after joining the Council. Both countries now claim to have abandoned the death penalty.

Extradition and refugees

Many countries have **extradition** agreements with others. This means that someone wanted for committing a crime in another country may be sent back there to stand trial. If a prisoner is likely to face the death penalty, most countries that do not have a death penalty themselves will refuse to extradite him or her. Even a country that does have a death penalty may refuse to extradite a prisoner to a country where the death penalty is cruelly administered or used for minor crimes.

Refugees are people who have run away from their own country, often because of war or poverty. If they make it as far as a developed Western country, they are usually allowed to stay if they can show that they will be persecuted, **tortured** or put to death if forced to return.

Lobbying

Pressure does not only come from other governments – individual citizens can make a difference, too.

Lobbying is the process of trying to persuade politicians to act in a particular way. It involves providing information and arguments to promote a cause. International and local organizations lobby for the abolition or restriction of the death penalty and for humane treatment of **condemned** prisoners. There are many charities that take an interest in the conditions in prisons and on death row around the world.

Amnesty International

The worldwide organization Amnesty International monitors the use of the death penalty and conditions on death row in many countries. It tries to work with governments to make sure people are treated fairly and well looked after. It takes on individual cases and campaigns on the behalf of people it believes have been unfairly convicted, or who are facing cruel and unjust treatment. It uses high-profile publicity campaigns to put pressure on governments to abolish the death penalty completely.

Pro- and anti-death penalty movements

Countries that have a death penalty often have groups campaigning to have it abolished. Some countries that have got rid of the death penalty, or are considering doing so, have groups campaigning to keep or reinstate it. In countries with harsh regimes, where the death penalty is widely used and prisoners are treated badly, openly

A protestor against the death penalty from Amnesty International shows a picture of a woman convicted of drug trafficking and about to be executed in China.

joining a movement for reform can itself be a crime, so people are not free to object and campaign. For them, international pressure is crucial.

The growth of the World Wide Web and email has led to a shift in how campaigning groups operate. People can become involved more easily and mass communication has become quick and cheap. It is easier, too, for a campaigning organization to operate internationally. For instance, recent petitions have collected names by email from around the world to protest against individual executions in Nigeria. High-speed international communications also make it harder for a regime to keep its **human rights** abuses hidden from the outside world – although many such places restrict people's access to information technology.

Could it happen to you?

Capital punishment may affect any of us, whether or not we live in a country that has the death penalty. There have been several cases recently of people visiting a country with a death penalty and ending up on death row. Some claim to be innocent of any crime; others have admitted to crimes which may carry the death penalty.

Tourists face execution

In recent years several Australian and European tourists have been imprisoned and some have faced execution for smuggling drugs into or out of Thailand, Singapore and Malaysia. Some of them have claimed that drugs were planted on them or that they carried them

without realising, and some admitted the charge. Usually, their own governments press the local authorities to reduce the sentences to imprisonment but this does not always work. Tourists convicted of a crime that carries the death penalty are subject to local law wherever they are travelling.

US emergency regulations put in place by the Executive Military Order (2001) after the attacks of 11 September 2001 allow the arrest, imprisonment and even execution of any foreign national suspected of terrorist activity. People may be arrested and tried by a special US military court anywhere in the world and have no right of **appeal**.

Terrorism suspects held at the US naval base at Guantanamo Bay, Cuba are not protected by the Geneva Convention or US law.

Australian Holly Deane-Johns escaped the death penalty after being cleared of trafficking drugs in Thailand, but other foreign nationals have been executed.

Case study Condemned in Thailand

Holly Deane-Johns was 29 when arrested in Thailand after trying to post 11 grams of heroin to her home in Australia. A further 15 grams were found in her apartment and 110 grams in her boyfriend's home. This put the total over the limit for mandatory execution for trafficking under Thai law.

She spent three years in Klong Prem Prison in Bangkok, known for the appalling conditions in which prisoners are kept. At her trial in 2003 she was cleared of drug trafficking and convicted instead of the lesser crime of possession and sentenced to 31 years in prison. She hopes to return to Australia for part of her sentence as she will be eligible for transfer under a treaty between Thailand and Australia.

Getting your voice heard

Do you feel strongly about capital punishment? Perhaps you live in a country with a death penalty that you feel should be abolished, or that you feel should be kept. Or maybe you live in a country that no longer has a death penalty but you feel it should be reinstated. Maybe you are happy with the state of your own country but concerned about unfair trials and cruel treatment in some other countries. What can you do about it?

Finding out more

Find out about the law in your own country or state. Is there a death penalty? If so, for which crimes? How many people are awaiting execution? Are they likely to be executed? You can find out more details by writing to, or looking on the website of, the government of your state or your local correctional institution.

Keep ahead of developments around the world by checking newspapers and reliable news sites on the web. Try http://news.bbc.co.uk, www.abc.net.au/news/ or www.cnn.com.

Working with organizations

There are many organizations that campaign to monitor or improve conditions for **condemned** prisoners around the world. There are also bodies working towards the abolition of the death penalty both globally and in individual countries. You will find the details of some of these organizations on page 52. They will be happy to provide you with information about their work and tell you how you can get involved if you want to do more.

In March 2002 Nigerian woman Amina Lawal was convicted of adultery and sentenced to death by stoning. Following international protests, her sentence was quashed and she was freed.

Individual cases

Throughout the world there are people who have been unfairly convicted and are sentenced to death. You can make a difference by writing to your local government representative and perhaps to officials in the country where a person is imprisoned. Amnesty International has a list of people wrongfully convicted and unfairly treated whom it is trying to help. Contact details for Amnesty International are on page 52.

There are petitions that you can 'sign' on the Web to add your name to the list of supporters for some individual cases. International support for Nigerian women sentenced to death by stoning has led to some sentences being overturned.

Consumer pressure

Economic pressure can make a difference, too. If you do not approve of how condemned prisoners are treated somewhere, you could make an effort not to buy goods from that country, and not to visit as a tourist.

Facts and figures

Execution methods worldwide

Method	Location
Shooting	73 countries including USA (only method in 45 countries)
Hanging	58 countries including USA (only method in 33 countries)
Stoning	Afghanistan, Iran, Nigeria, Pakistan, Saudi Arabia, Sudan, United Arab Emirates
Lethal injection	China, Guatemala (only method), Philippines, Taiwan, Thailand, USA
Beheading	Iran, Saudi Arabia, United Arab Emirates, Congo (but abolitionist in practice)
Electrocution	USA
Lethal gas	USA

Execution in the USA

A total of 877 executions were carried out in the USA between the reintroduction of the death penalty in 1976 (see page 39) and the beginning of October 2003. Of these, 710 were by lethal injection, 151 by electrocution, 11 by gas chamber, 3 by hanging and 2 by shooting.

The state that carries out most executions is Texas, which carried out 33 of the 71 executions in 2002. This is followed by Oklahoma (seven executions) and Missouri (six executions). One of the executions was by electrocution and the other 70 by lethal injection. Two of those executed were women and 69 were men.

Timeline of abolition

1066	England: death penalty in peace time abolished by William the Conqueror; it was reintroduced by his son, William II
1468	San Marino (small republic in Southern Europe): last execution – the first country to give up the death penalty
1786	Tuscany (now part of Italy): abolition
1834	USA: Pennsylvania became the first state to stop public executions
1846	USA: Michigan abolished the death penalty for all crimes except **treason**
1863	Venezuela: abolition – the first country to abolish the death penalty formally and not reinstate it
1865	San Marino: formal abolition
1868	Britain: last public hangings in England and Scotland
1875	Britain: last public hanging in British Isles (Jersey)
1964	Britain: last execution
1965	Britain: death penalty effectively abolished, except for treason
1967	Australia: last execution
1972	USA: The Supreme Court ruled the death penalty **unconstitutional** and it was suspended in all states that still had it
1976	Canada: abolition in civil law
1976	USA: The Supreme Court approved re-worded laws in several states, allowing the death penalty to be reinstated
1984	UN ruled against the execution of anyone under eighteen years of age at the time of committing their crime
1985	Australia: abolition
1989	New Zealand: abolition
1993	International War Crimes Tribunal ruled against death penalty in all cases
1998	Canada: total abolition
1999	Britain: death penalty abolished completely after the European Convention on **Human Rights** is incorporated into British law
2002	Council of Europe requires complete abolition of the death penalty in all member states under all circumstances; this is the first legally binding international treaty abolishing capital punishment

Further information

Contacts

Background information

The Death Penalty Information Center
www.deathpenaltyinfo.org
A site with lots of information on the death penalty in the USA.

Capital Punishment UK
www.richard.clark32.btinternet.co.uk
Information about the death penalty in the UK up to 1964.

Texas Department of Criminal Justice
www.tdcj.state.tx.us/stat/deathrow.htm
Includes information on prisoners on death row in Texas, USA.

Florida Department of Corrections
www.dc.state.fl.us/oth/deathrow/
Includes information on prisoners on death row in Florida, USA.

Trinity College, Western Australia
http://library.trinity.wa.edu.au/issues/
capital.htm
A site on issues relating to the death penalty with lots of links to useful sites.

For and against

Even if you think you have already made your mind up about the death penalty, it is worth looking at the arguments from the other side of the debate, too.

Death Penalty Focus
www.deathpenalty.org
Against the death penalty in the USA.

Australian Coalition Against the Death Penalty
http://acadp.com/
An anti-death-penalty group in Australia.

World Coalition Against the Death Penalty
http://www.worldcoalition.org/
The website of an anti-capital-punishment group founded in Rome, Italy in 2002.

Legislation

The United Nations
www.un.org
Go to **www.un.org/Overview/brief.html** for an outline of the UN's work and aims.

Helping prisoners

Amnesty International UK
99–119 Rosebery Avenue
London EC1R 4RE
Tel: 020 7814 6200
email: info@amnesty.org.uk
www.amnesty.org.uk

Amnesty International USA
322 Eighth Avenue
New York, NY 10001
Tel: (212) 807-8400
www.amnestyusa.org
Amnesty International works to reform conditions on death row everywhere, to have the death penalty abolished everywhere and to help individuals suffering from injustice around the world.

Fair Trials Abroad
Bench House, Ham Street
Richmond, Surrey TW10 7HR, UK
Tel: 020 7981 0415
www.f-t-a.freeserve.co.uk
Helps EU citizens facing imprisonment or death abroad.

Human Rights Watch
350 Fifth Avenue, 34th floor
New York, NY 10118-3299 USA
Tel: (212) 290-4700
email: hrwnyc@hrw.org

2nd Floor, 2–12 Pentonville Road
London N1 9HF, UK
Tel: 020 7713 1995
email: hrwuk@hrw.org
www.hrw.org

Human Rights Watch defends human rights around the world.

Further reading

The books below are suitable for older readers:

Beyond Repair?: America's Death Penalty, S Garvey ed. (Duke University Press, 2003)

Dead Man Walking: An Eyewitness Account of the Death Penalty in the United States, Sister Helen Prejean (Random House, 1994)

The Death Penalty: A Worldwide Perspective, Roger Hood (Oxford University Press, 2002)

The Hanging Tree: Execution and the English People, V A C Gatrell (Oxford Paperbacks, 1996)

Machinery of Death: The Reality of America's Death Penalty Regime, David R Dow and Mark Dow (Routledge Inc, 2002)

Reflections on the Guillotine, in *Resistance, Rebellion and Death*, Albert Camus, translated by Justin O'Brien (Vintage Books, 1995)

❝If we execute murderers and there is in fact no deterrent effect, we have killed a bunch of murderers. If we fail to execute murderers, and doing so would in fact have deterred other murders, we have allowed the killing of a bunch of innocent victims. I would much rather risk the former.❞

John McAdams – Department of Political Science, Marquette University, Milwaukee, USA

Glossary

adultery
sex between a married person and someone who is not their wife or husband

appeals
judicial hearings after a person's first trial at which they and their lawyers try to have their conviction or sentence changed. They may bring new evidence, or argue that the first trial was unfair or improper in some way.

atrocities
crimes involving inflicting physical suffering on people

capital offence
crime for which the criminal can be sentenced to death

closure
feeling that an episode in life is complete and the person can move on to other things

condemned
person who has had a death sentence passed on them

conviction
being found guilty of a crime

corporal punishment
physical punishment for a crime or misbehaviour

death row
special part of a prison where condemned prisoners are held

defendant
person arguing in court against an accusation that they have committed a crime

desertion
running away from battle

discretionary death sentence
death sentence that may be passed if someone is convicted of a particular crime, but the judge can decide to inflict another punishment instead

DNA
deoxyribonucleic acid, the chemical substance that contains information in the form of genes. Each person's DNA is unique, and criminals may be identified from DNA (in blood, hair or skin, for example) left at a crime scene.

extradition
sending a convicted or suspected criminal back to the country in which they are wanted for a crime

federal
relating to the whole confederation of American states, rather than to specific states

federal law
law in the USA that applies to the whole Union rather than to individual states

firing squad
group of marksmen who all shoot at a condemned prisoner at the same time. Not all the guns may contain live ammunition.

fraud
deliberately falsifying documents or procedures in order to obtain something, usually money, unfairly

gallows
scaffold for hanging condemned prisoners

genocide
illegal mass killing of a national or ethnic group of people with the aim of destroying that group

gibbet
metal cage hung from a scaffold or frame and containing the body of an executed prisoner

guillotine
device with a falling blade for beheading condemned prisoners

heinous
very serious

heretics
people whose religious beliefs are counter to those supported by the Church

human rights
rights that are deemed to apply to all people around the world. They cover basic entitlements such as freedom from slavery, access to clean water and sufficient food, essential healthcare and education.

intelligence quotient (IQ)
numerical score achieved on special tests designed to test intelligence

intravenous
administered directly into the blood vessels (into a vein)

IRA (Irish Republican Army)
military organization working for political independence of Northern Ireland from the UK

judicial
involving a court of law

jury
group of people from the population who debate and decide whether a person accused of a crime is guilty or innocent

legal code
system of laws

mandatory death sentence
death sentence which must be passed if someone is convicted of a particular crime – no other sentence is allowed

marksmen
soldiers or executioners who use guns to carry out an execution

non-custodial punishment
a punishment that does not involve being held in prison

parole
early release from a prison sentence

regime
controlling political group or system in a state

stay of execution
delay of an execution that has been scheduled, usually for further consideration of arguments or evidence

strip-search
to search someone for hidden items – often drugs or weapons – by removing all their clothes and often checking body cavities

torture
illegal use of physical, emotional or mental violence, usually intended to persuade someone to do or say something against their will

treason
deliberately acting to overthrow or undermine the ruling government, or against the interests of one's country

unconstitutional
contrary to a state's constitution (regulations that set down how the state must be run)

United Nations (UN)
international body set up in 1945 to promote international peace and cooperation

Index

Titles in the *Just the Facts* series include:

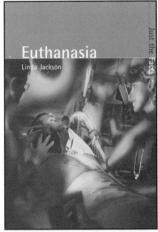

Hardback   0 431 16174 7

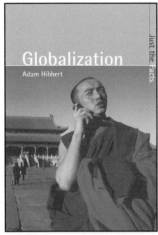

Hardback   0 431 16175 5

Hardback   0 431 16176 3

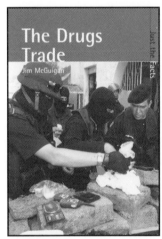

Hardback   0 431 16177 1

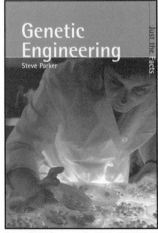

Hardback   0 431 16178 X

Hardback   0 431 16179 8

Find out about the other titles in this series on our website www.heinemann.co.uk/library